DAY TRADING
FOR
BEGINNERS

Find Out All the Basics and the
Right Tips to Become a Established
Day Trader. A Simple Beginner's
Guide to Making Real Money Daily
and Quitting Your 9-to-5 Job.

DAVE ROBERT WARREN GRAHAM

IPH BOOKS
INVESTING AND TRADING ACADEMY

Published by IPH Books - "Investing and Trading Academy" Collection
♦ All rights reserved, including the right of reproduction in whole or in part in any form ♦

ISBN: [978-1914409462] Paperback Black&White
ISBN: [978-1914409479] Paperback Color 2nd edition
ISBN: [978-1914409486] Hardcover Black&White
ISBN: [978-1914409493] Hardcover Color 2nd edition

Success is not the key to happiness. Happiness is the key to success. If you love what you are doing, you will be successful.

If you love Day trading consistently then you will be successful up in this amazing business. I love to look at the charts daily, open 2 or 3 trades per day and take profit at the end of the day... every day! You don't need that much time per day to be successful with day trading, you just need consistency, apply the right strategies and never deviate from your plan. Day trading has changed my life and I hope it will change yours. From this book, you will have everything you need to understand and get started in day trading.

Good luck with your reading and studies

Dave R. W. Graham

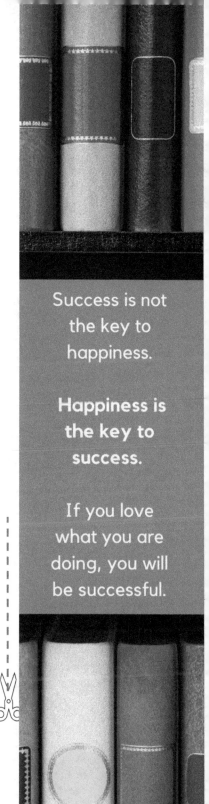

Success is not the key to happiness.

Happiness is the key to success.

If you love what you are doing, you will be successful.

Success is not
the key to
happiness.

**Happiness is
the key to
success.**

If you love
what you are
doing, you will
be successful.

Table of Content

Introduction

All over the world, stock markets open in the morning. Those day traders who think they can start trading while munching on their breakfast, with no preparation, are among those who make losses. All businesses open in the morning. No successful businessman just gets up, yawns, and starts his business activities. Successful professionals arrive in their office with a clear idea of how they will tackle the work and related challenges.

Likewise, to succeed in day trading, one must prepare beforehand. These preparations include many aspects, such as mental, physical, emotional, and financial. Professional traders have clear advice for day traders: never trade if you are tired or stressed, never trade if you are feeling highly emotional, and trade with clear money management concepts.

Day trading is a sophisticated business activity, where people try to earn money by using their intelligence. Therefore, physical or emotional stress can cause harm to your trading business. You will not be able to make rational decisions if you are tired or feeling stressed. Before you start the day's trading, you should be physically, mentally, and emotionally alert. A good night's sleep is necessary for traders to tackle the roller coaster ride of stock markets. Here are a few steps that will help you prepare for day trading with a cool temperament and calm mind. Before going to sleep, keep your trading plan ready. Check the stock chart, make notes on the chart what big patterns the price created in the previous session. Note down the important support and resistance levels. Then mentally go over this chart and imagine how you will trade in the next session in different trend conditions.

Do not spend too much time watching the news about stock markets or anything else. Watching the news may create doubts in your mind about stock trends and influence your decision-making power for the next session. If possible, do some breathing exercises or meditation before going to sleep, which will sharpen your focusing power and reduce stress.

Also, prepare your money-plans for the next trading session. How much will you invest? What will be your loss tolerance level? And what will be your profit booking point? During the trading hours, these decisions must be made in a split second, and if you are already prepared, you will not hesitate to make the right decision.

These will also help you set your goals for intraday trading. Just stick to your goals and you will not face any decision-making problems during the trading hours.

The final stage of your preparation will be an hour before the markets open in the morning. This is the time when you check the news reports about the business and financial world, and the economic calendar. By doing so, you will know what events could influence that day's trading pattern in the stock market. You can also check how the world markets are trading in that session. Sometimes all markets trade in one direction, which will be beneficial to know before your local stock markets open.

In day trading, financial instruments are bought and sold within the same session. Sometimes more than once through the same day. To be successful in this endeavor, traders need to know where the price might make important moves. Technical charts are very helpful tools in deciphering this price moment. Anybody involved in stock trading relies heavily on stock charts, which is why successful traders always create their trading plans before making any trading decisions.

Day trading is a demanding profession and requires significant time. Any market session runs for at least 6 hours a day, and you will have to spend that much time watching and observing markets, even if not reading. Apart from trading hours, a day trader needs to research, create trading plans, and keep learning new things. All these require time and effort.

Therefore, to succeed in day trading, you will need to manage your time effectively. Usually, people want to adopt a day trading career so they will have working flexibility. This means freedom from getting up early and rushing to get caught in the morning traffic, freedom from having a boss, and of course, financial freedom. Nothing comes easy in this world. A dream life also requires putting in lots of effort. Many day traders find it difficult to complete their trading routines, such as after-hours research and planning. Part-time traders who are already busy with some other work also struggle to prepare for day trading in their spare time.

Chapter 1.

What is Day Trading?

Topic Covered:

♦ Trading in Stocks

♦ Trading in Forex

♦ Trading in Futures

D ay trading is the demonstration of trading on the stock market during the day. Foreign countries are locked in with the exchange to publicize also. When we are hitting the sack, those nations that are awakening imply that there is a different side to the market that numerous individuals don't consider. In any case, for the time being, how about we worry about the nuts and bolts.

The key point of convergence of day trading is to purchase and offer a stock inside one day to make a benefit. This isn't the main technique for trading. Many day traders are doing this now with the internet. Internet trading is the same thing as trading in person. You get the same stocks, at the same prices, at the same time. That is why many people are moving out of the stock market and onto the internet. This is especially useful in day trading because it executes your purchases and sales instantly. When you are dealing with stocks that are moving fractions of a point, being able to complete a transaction immediately is extremely important.

There are many places that you can get information to help you find the answer to what is day trading. Online sources can offer you a wealth of information. There are also trade schools that can help you get started. Many schools provide seminars. Some schools even offer all-day lessons that can get you caught up on all the latest stock market news, techniques, and trends.

If you should be a compelling seller, you need to get data about the market. The more information you have, the better your chances are to acquire money. It is a very complicated market, and you need to be tuned to the current market trends. Staying informed can help you when it comes time to make decisions about your stocks. Day trading can be a very lucrative activity if you know how to do it right. Why day trade? Is it worth the effort? Day exchanging offers the way to financial opportunity.

You shouldn't be incredibly keen to be successful in day exchanging. The best day traders are the individuals who have iron-resolve and robust order. Intelligence is unquestionably invited yet isn't a fundamental basis for progress. I was never the top in my group and consistently scratched through my tests. Exchanging takes an alternate way to deal with bring in money. The period considered is short from a couple of moments to hours to days, weeks, or perhaps a month. Day exchanging alludes to carefully transferring inside the day. This implies you don't hold positions for the time being. For example: if you buy at 10:00 (EST), you need to sell before 16:15(EST) when the market closes.

There are no standards against holding, for the time being, nevertheless, the hazard is limited if exchanging is carefully confined to inside the day. The market regularly moves in response to the news when exchanges are shut. Stocks generally don't have a lot of liquidity and trade on light volume secondary selling hours. Envision what might befall your long position when there is a sudden tropical storm strike when the market is shut.

The market will drop, yet you probably won't have the option to sell at a sensible price because of low volume. Whatever losses and rewards are exacting during market hours when there is enough volume to trade.

Trading in Stocks

The thought of trading in stocks scares away many investors. Individuals who have never traded are terrified by the fact that one can easily lose money with wrong decisions. The reality is, stock trading is a risky activity. However, when approached with the right market knowledge, it is an efficient way of building your net worth.

It is a financial instrument which amounts to ownership in a company. When an individual purchases a stock or shares, it means that they own a portion or fraction of the company. For instance, say a trader owns 10,000 shares in a company with 100,000 shares.

This would mean that the individual has 10% ownership of the stakes. The buyer of such shares is identified as a shareholder. Therefore, the more shares one owns, the larger the proportion of the company which they own.

Every time the value of the company shares rise, your share value will also rise. Similarly, if the value falls, your share value also declines. When a company makes a profit, the shareholders are also bestowed with the profits in the form of dividends.

Preferred stock and common stock are the two main types of stocks you should be aware of. The difference that lies between these stocks is that with common stocks, it carries voting rights.

This means that a shareholder influences company meetings. Hence, they can have a say in company meetings where the board of directors is elected. On the other hand, preferred shares lack voting rights.

However, they are identified as "preferred" shares or stocks because of their preference over common stocks. If a company goes through liquidation, shareholders with preferred shares will be preferred to receive assets or dividends.

Trading in Forex

Most traders would argue that trading in the forex is quite complicated. However, it's not. Just like any other form of trading, you must stick to the basic rules. In this case, you need to buy when the market is rising and ensure you sell when the market is dropping.

Trading in forex involves the process of trading in currencies. In simpler terms, a trader exchanges currency for others based on certain agreed rates. If you have traveled to foreign countries and exchanged your currency against their local currencies, you should understand how trading in forex works.

At first, it could seem confusing to choose the best currencies, but a trader should simply go for major currencies. Some of the frequently traded currencies include the U.S. dollar, Japanese

Limit your trading to the markets you know well and leave the rest alone.

Yen, European Union Euro, Australian dollar, Canadian dollar, and Swiss franc. An important thing you ought to understand about forex trading is that you need to trade in pairs.

This means that when you are buying one currency, you should do this while simultaneously selling another. If you do some digging, you will notice that currencies are quoted in pairs, i.e., USD/JPY or EUR/USD. Below is an image showing how currencies are quoted in pairs.

Trading in Futures

Most traders prefer to trade in futures due to their associated advantages. Trading in futures is quite flexible and diverse. The good news is that a trader can employ almost any methodology to trade. Some traders shy away from this form of trading due to their limited knowledge about futures. Also, others are discouraged from trading in futures because they think that it is difficult.

Well, to some extent, this is true. Comparing trading in futures to trading in stocks, the former is very risky. There are different forms of futures contracts, including currencies, energies, interest rates, metals, food sector futures, and agricultural futures. The best futures contracts you will find in the market are briefly in the following lines:

- **S&P 500 E-mini:** Most traders will fancy the idea of trading in the S&P 500 E-mini because of its high liquidity aspect. It also appeals to most investors because of its low day trading margins. You can conveniently trade in S&P 500 E-mini around the clock, not to mention that you will also benefit from its technical analysis aspect. Essentially, the S&P 500 E-mini is a friendly contract since you can easily predict its price patterns.

- **10 Year T-Notes:** 10 Year T-Notes is also ranked as one of the best contracts to trade-in. Considering its sweet maturity aspect, most traders would not hesitate to trade in this futures contract. There are low margin requirements that a trader will have to meet when trading in 10 Year T-Notes.

- **Crude Oil:** Crude oil also stands as one of the most popular commodities in futures trading. It is an exciting market because of its high daily trading volume of about 800k. Its high volatility also makes the market highly lucrative.

- **Gold:** This is yet another notable futures contract. It might be expensive to trade in gold, however, it is a great hedging choice more so in poor market conditions.

- **Trading in Stock Options:** Trading in stock options is almost like trading in futures. Here, a trader also buys stocks at a pre-established price and later sells when prices rise.

- **Capital Requirements:** Stock options trading also affected by the Pattern Day Trading Rule. This means that your minimum capital requirements will be $25,000. If you engage in more than four trades in a week, you should have about $30,000 in your trading account.

- **Leverage:** Since there are many options to choose from, leverage will vary. The exciting aspect of stock options is that they have high leverage amounts.

- **Liquidity:** Regarding liquidity, stock options are not that liquid. A keen eye on this market reveals that a few options are traded regularly. The low volume of trades is affected by the many options that traders can choose from. Fortunately, stock options are rarely manipulated by the market. Their values are not influenced by supply and demand.

- **Volatility:** Stock options are highly volatile.

From the look of things, stock options have similar pros and cons, like trading in stocks. Most new traders will shy away from this form of day trading due to its high capital demands. Its high volatility could be scary to most investors as it makes the market to be unpredictable.

This makes this form of trading to be very risky. Therefore, it is not recommended for new traders.

Chapter 2.

Pros and Cons of Day Trading

Topic Covered:

♦ Pro and Cons

Pros

- **You want to earn profits at the end of the day:** The idea that it is a "get rich quick" scheme may be part truth since you do get to earn a profit after the market closes. For example: let us pretend that you invested $100 for 100 shares. The market fluctuation is in your favor, so when you sell it, you double your money, which means you now have revenue of $2 per share—not too shabby, right?

- **You want to think less about your investments:** This is because once the market closes, your trading also ends. Whether you win or lose, that is left to your skill and fate. The main point is that you will not have to think about whether your stock value will fall the next day or whether US dollar is going to be strong in the following week. You think day by day, moment by moment.

- **You can build cash inflow and liquidity very quickly:** This can be related to the first point. Because you can earn revenues and profits by the end of the day, you can also boost your assets, which then means you can buy more securities and increase your chance of earning more money in a short period of time. I highly encourage that you diversify your portfolio even if they belong to the same class (e.g., class of stocks) to protect yourself in deep market fluctuations, which are not that common anyway.

- **You are better protected against market fluctuations:** Diversification can help shield you from deep fluctuations in the market. But here is something to be happy about: the likelihood that it is going to dip extremely low is very small. As expected, market prices can change very fast in a blink of an eye, but the movements are often small.

- **You can be your own boss:** As a retail trader, you call the shots. You decide how much to invest, where to put your money, when to buy or sell, how much you like to earn, the securities you like to trade, etc.

- **You have help:** You may be a beginner, but the learning curve is not as difficult as it is with other securities or types of investing or trading. A variety of materials are available to make sure you do not have to trade blindly.

Cons

- **It requires a lot of time:** All types of work or endeavor needs it. Although there are specific hours of the day when you trade best, you still must be alert if the market stays open because you will never really know what is going to happen. Stock prices could plunge, which gives you the perfect moment to buy blue chips or those that you can't afford before. If the European forex session is bad, there is a good chance US session will suffer the same fate as well. It is almost the same scenario when we talk about other securities like bonds, hedge contracts, futures, or commodities. Let us not forget too that you would have to do your research after or in between trading.

- **It is risky:** To be honest, life is all about and related to risk. You are surrounded by it. When you cross the road or drive the car, you run the risk of meeting an accident. When you sleep, there is still a good chance you will never wake up! Have you heard of the term idiopathic? In science, it means a disease, or a condition that happens with no known or determined cause. It is simply saying it occurred just because it can.

The levels of risks we face daily, however, can vary. In the world of day trading, it can be on opposite ends, depending on how you trade and how much you put in. The bigger the money, the bigger the possible loss. The higher the returns, the higher the chance of falling hard. Losing is all part of the game. The problem comes in if you lose everything—that is a possibility, you know.

- **It can make you emotional:** You can blame it on pressure, sense of competition, pride, or whatever. Whether you like it or not, day trading can get to you, and in many days, it is not a pleasant activity to do.

The relationship between emotions and commerce is strong. Many studies have already shown that customers are more likely to buy items on impulse and buy products that capture their emotions. The theory or concept of scarcity to sell something is also based on emotion.

By instilling fear—the idea that if they do not act fast, they can no longer take advantage of the offer—is what has earned several businesspeople millions or even billions of dollars.

You can, therefore, not avoid being emotional, whether it is positive or negative when you are trading. However, you should learn how to control it and/or decrease its influence and impact on your decisions.

It can make you complacent: These days, it is so easy to get confident or even cocky with day trading. After all, you have more tools and resources compared to many years ago. You even have auto programs that can do the trading for you just in case you want to have some 'me time' in the middle of the day. But complacency can be one of your biggest mistakes. As you relax, that is when you become least prepared for the uncertainties.

Your software can bog down, the analyses it provides you can be wrong, markets go down quickly without you knowing it—these things you could have resolved to minimize the effect on you only if you have paid attention and be more proactive or do your part.

- **There are fees:** A lot of people think that they can just trade for free. Of course, it does not work that way. You have different expenses and fees to pay, including commissions for every execution (e.g., buying or selling). And there are tax implications. You still must pay your taxes because you are getting some profit from the transaction. In fact, taxes are higher for short-term investments such as those of day trading than the ones held for a long time, which is at least a year. But the good news is there are caps set. Also, if you're having a loss, you can write it off up to the amount of your capital gains.

To be successful in trading and investing you must be prepared to fail.

So that you can be prepared to win without losing your head.

Chapter 3.

Tips and Tricks Used for Day Trading

Topic Covered:

- Have a Plan with You
- Use Demo Accounts
- Have a Routine for Day Trading?
- Never Get Tired of Learning
- Be Responsible
- Shun Losses

- Set Your Entry Point
- Set Realistic ProfitsHave a Strong Trust for Yourself?
- Learn from Experience
- Be Calm, Take Control of Your Greed

Develop a Good Attitude

D ay trading requires you to learn the tips and tricks for you to ace it. Many are the traders who fail to finish through day trading because they failed to follow on the few tips and tricks or had no idea of them. For you to be an expert in something, it is a prerequisite to be a beginner. Below are the few tips and tricks to employ in day trading for you to succeed.

Have a Plan with You

A trading plan is a set of policies that guides a trader on its activities. It is a necessary tool needed by all individuals. You always need to have a plan for everything you are working on. As a beginner in day trading, you also need to plan on how to do your trading.

A plan entails how, when, and why to do your day trading. It will guide you on what action to implement to attain a certain number of sales or even profits for your trading. A trading plan will alert you when you are on the wrong path, and you will be able to correct yourself so quickly before it is too late.

Make Use of Demo Accounts

Most day trading software normally provides mock accounts for their traders. You should take full advantage of them. Before getting into the real accounts, practice trading with the demo accounts, but they provide virtual cash.

They also provide tools such as charts which you can read on the price fluctuations. Charts improve the performance of a trader a lot. Know the tricks in trading using these accounts and perfect your skills. After that, you can confidently create a real account with a broker and ace day trading.

Have a Routine for Day Trading?

Have yourself a routine on how to do your trading. Routine is a set of scheduled activities for any individual. Evaluate your market trades effectively and efficiently and make sure they align with your trading plan.

Scheduling yourself will make you organized, and you will be able to correct the mistakes that may arise.

Never Get Tired of Learning

Trading keeps evolving with time. As a trader, you should not be left behind. Be alert with all that is evolving. Do a lot of research, learn from articles and videos, and be alert with the trends in trading? Study on the price fluctuations to be up to date.

Big losses and market risks will affect you when you stop learning. Though do not overwork yourself to research everything all at once. Go at your speed and have the basic knowledge on day trading.

Be Responsible

Responsibility and self-discipline are a must to succeed in day trading. What I mean by being responsible is by taking the correct actions on the mistakes that arise and learn from the mistakes. Never ignore the mistakes, you will fail.

Also, make sure that what you do is what is included in your trading plan. If it is still not working out, go back to your trading plan. Make changes to it and try again. By doing this, your day trading business will have no complications and issues.

Begin with Little Cash

Do not be so overexcited when starting day trading. Day trading involves lots of risks, and not being careful with trading risks can make you fail terribly. When starting day trading, begin with little cash. Using lots of cash as a beginner can contribute to huge risks to the business.

Little and reliable cash guarantees you with good profits, unlike risking a lot of your money, and end up losing. Always remember this trick to succeed in day trading.

> Profit does not come from a particular winning investment, but from a series of winning and losing investments

Shun Losses

Losses are everywhere. They can be a nuisance sometimes in business when they occur. Some manage to be cautious enough to beat these losses, but they end up just giving up for the faint-hearted. I do not want this to happen to you as a beginner in day trading.

In day trading, you need to weigh and select the securities that are safe for you. If a market trade does not benefit you, leave it and look for the one that is good for you. This will enable you to shun the losses in day trading.

Utilize Resources

You need to take advantage of the resources provided to you by the brokers. The resources can be research tools, and news feeds, tools for analysis, charting tools, and backtesting tools—select software with abundant tools for easier trading. Research as much as possible to be up to date.

Read and follow up the charts to have good data on the prices fluctuating in the market. Also, utilize the news. News will keep on updating you on the market changes in terms of the prices of the securities.

Analyze the different markets with the tools provided. Weigh options and select the best market you can handle.

Have the Basics for Day Trading?

The basics for day trading include a good Internet connection, a stable trading platform, a cheaper, and a legit broker and try your best and own a desktop or a laptop.

Purchase for yourself a strong Internet, be it wired or wireless connection. This will promote fast and good quality trade executions. It will also save you a lot of time. Slow Internet will slow down your trade executions, and you will not be up to date on the market changes.

A trader is advised to have at least two desktops. You can have one laptop at the start if money is an issue but having two monitors is the most advised one. If one of the desktop crashes at crucial moments while trading, you would at least have a backup, and you will lose no profit. Having one monitor can be so risky and will affect your trading performance.

Trading platforms are essential for all-day traders. Select a trading platform which is of ease of use. Choose software with a friendly user interface since you spend your time mostly in here. Also, consider the cost and stability of the platform. Unstable trading platforms can crash down anytime, and you will lose all your profits and data.

Choosing platforms that are expensive for you to afford is a very bad idea. Select the software with the cost that you are comfortable with to avoid spending much than the profit. Also, select a trading platform with enough tools. The tools will ease the trading process and will increase your performance.

A day trading broker can be legit or fake. Know how to distinguish the two. Be aware of the legit brokers and make a connection with them. Choose a legal broker with reliable software and less commission. Some brokers can be hard on you by charging a high commission on your trades.

You need to put your profits into consideration since the main aim of all businesses is to make a profit. Also, select a trading broker near you or within the same country so you can get assistance whenever you are in need.

Have a Schedule for Your Trades?

As a beginner, you need to sit down and have a schedule for the time you will be day trading. Different markets have different times of trading. It depends on the type of trading you are working on. Here is a schedule for Forex, stock, and future types of trading.

For Forex traders, you can trade within 24 hours. Though the best time to trade in Forex markets is around 6.00 am and 5.00 pm GMT.

For the stock traders, the best time to trade comes in two ranges of time. You can decide to wake up early, and trade around 9.30 am—1.30 pm EST or around 1500hours-1600hours EST.

For futures traders, the appropriate time for your trade is around 8.30 am—11.00 pm EST.

So be aware of the best time to make your trades to grab the best opportunities. Do not just trade anytime you feel like it.

Set Your Entry Point

Identifying your entry and exit points is a crucial thing to consider as a beginner in day trading. An entry point is a trader's price to purchase or sell a market trade, whereas an exit point is its vice versa.

A trader should ensure there is a big difference between an entry and an exit point to promote growth in trading.

Set Realistic Profits

Do not set high-profit targets, and you are just a beginner. Set reasonable profits that are realistic to achieve with little experience in trading. Focus on how to improve your trading skills and perfect them. Trading needs patience, so relax and do it the right way. Do not rush. Beginners who rush for bigger profits end up failing in trading.

Have a Strong Trust for Yourself?

Trusting yourself is a crucial necessity for any trader. Trust the process you are facing, and all will be well. Do not over-read articles and watch too many videos, and you will lose hope during this journey. Have the one trading strategy you normally implement at your fingertips and do what you must do.

Learn from Experience

Losses are normal in businesses. Do not be a trader with a faint heart. When things do not turn out of what you expected, breathe in. Learn from the mistakes you made and improve next time. You will progress by learning from your mistakes. So, do it. Do not mind what others will tell you.

Be Calm

Do not panic or stress a lot when the stock market begins acting crazy. Be hopeful and courageous enough to handle it to be successful. Fear of failure should not be part of you. Do what you have scheduled yourself to do according to your trading plan, and all will be alright. Invest in other stuff in your life, do not focus too much on trading.

Take Control of Your Greed

Greed normally affects traders so much. For instance, you can make a trade of around $30 and set your profit target at $45. You, fortunately, hit this target at first trading. You then think of setting the target a bit higher to earn more, but unfortunately, you fail terribly for the second time, ending up making big losses.

My point here is that you need to be patient in trading. As time goes by, profits will increase. Set profit targets according to your trading plan and avoid losses.

Develop a Good Attitude

Day trading is not an easy thing. Many have lost hope and gave up on it, but you should not be part of them. Develop an amazingly positive and winning attitude that you will make it no matter what. Make sure to concentrate on what is to be done and what is according to your trading plan.

If you comply with these tips, day trading will not be tough for you.

Chapter 4.

Basics of Scalping

Topic Covered:

♦ Types of Scalping

A lways remember that personality determines the trading style. You don't do what others are doing. You do what will match your trading personality, style, and approach. When you're a position trader, your system is designed to take a long-term view of assets. When you switch to a scalping trading, your system might be suitable with that mode of trading.

However, a day trader can use scalping several times in a day. Generally, day trading involves holding positions for about thirty minutes or more. But scalping involves holding positions from seconds to even five minutes.

That is why many scalpers love reading and analyzing five-minute stock charts. It helps them to make good scalping decisions. A scalper cannot wait for several days before trading. He or she is an active trader, looking to make the most amount of profit in the market in the shortest possible time. Thus, a scalper engages in more trades than all the others of traders in a single trading session.

To get started with scalping, you need to understand the basics and how it works. Based on this definition, there are few things you must know: one, scalping focuses on "profiting off small price changes" and the second is that the seasoned scalpers simply focus on "a trade that has been executed and becomes profitable."

They do not worry about huge price changes in the market. A scalper makes trading easy because they lavage profitable trades to make profits.

Types of Scalping

Volatility, pricing, and volume are the three main factors that influenced how scalp trades are being placed. Before you proceed and start using scalping, you might as well learn a lot from about these critical elements of successful scalping. Not only do they affect scalping, but they also help to create the different types of scalping that exit in the financial market.

- **Less Volatile Security" Approach:** This type of scalping focuses on trading fewer volatile stocks with no real price changes, but they have high trading volume. Once there is a large trading volume, scalpers will then focus on capitalizing the spread to trade and make profits. This type of scalping is known as "market-making."

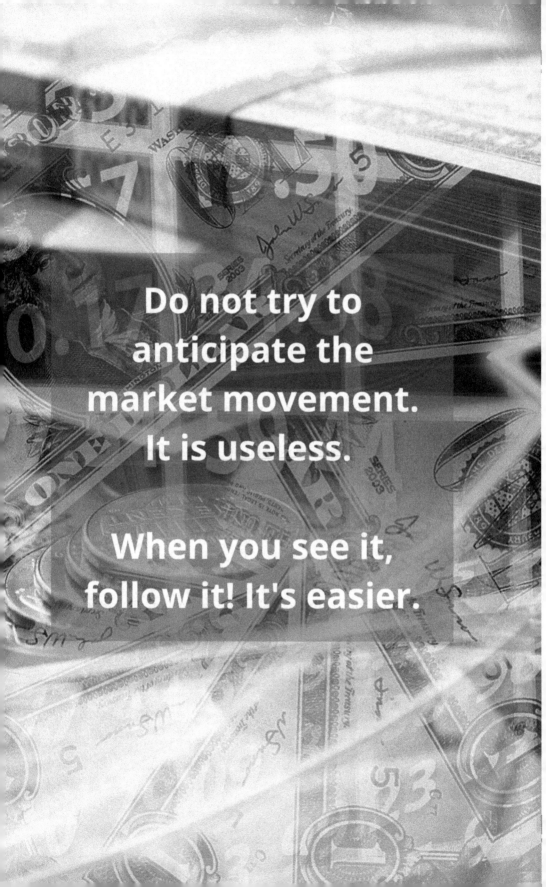

Do not try to anticipate the market movement. It is useless.

When you see it, follow it! It's easier.

In this approach, a scalper is trying to bet against the "market makers." It is executed by posting a bid and an offer on the same financial instrument simultaneously.

You level the price difference between the bid and the offer to quickly make money in the market. Analyzing the direction of the stock and volume is critical for success.

- **"Highly Volatile Security" Approach:** When the stock or a financial instrument is quickly moving, you can consider a trading approach that will tally with the volatility of the market. When the market is volatile, pricing will obviously be changing quickly, creating a perfect environment for scalp trading.

The idea here is to buy many shares and the bet against price movement. When the price moves slightly, the scalp will generate a profit and you will win. The stock must be liquid, and you need to evaluate and time the market well before trading. The focus is to wait for a small movement to make a profit.

- **"Close at Exit" Approach:** In the third trading approach, you use the same or similar trading as the second one. You try to make profits by waiting for a small change in prices of stocks or financial securities to make money. But here, you're more focused on your exit. Once the trade hits your exit strategy, you close the trade, take your profits and get out of the position.

With this approach, you need to analyze and develop an exit strategy that allows you to make the maximum from the scalp as well as reduce losses from market reversals.

Ideally, the risk/reward ratio for this kind of trade will be set at 1:1. A scalper operates with the belief that it is easy to capture profit from small prices changes in the financial market rather than wait for a large price moves to make a profit.

The accumulated profits from the small profits are what give scalpers the winning edge over long-term traders like position traders. To become a successful scalper, you need to have a specific way of thinking, behaving and acting.

If not, you will see yourself giving up before you succeed. No matter the kind of financial instrument you want to engage in through scalping, here are the top three psychological and behavioral patterns you must have.

- **Consistency:** Scalping can look very easy from the outside, but if you don't follow a trading system consistently, you're not going to make it. As a scalper, you're placing trades every few minutes and second. That means your trading must be carefully planned and organized to avoid disaster. If you do not, you will only waste your trading capital on useless stuff.

- **Discipline:** The decision-making system of a scalper is quite different from that of a swing trader and a day trader. You need to be brutally hard with yourself to be successful. When you reach a decision about a trading decision, you don't have time to be feeling and rehearsing. You must learn to independent decisions very quickly to enter and exit a trade.

- **Flexible:** While you must be hard on yourself, rugged and stiff with your trading plan and system, you need to also be flexible. Flexibility is necessary to respond to change that might occur in the market that might not be discoursed in your trading plan. When a trade is not going as you expect, just get out of the market and move on to the next trade.

- **Commitment to research:** A position trader needs an amount of research to trade, but scalping needs more. If you're scalping, you are placing more trade in a day and that requires you to do your homework on different kinds of securities before scalping. By so doing, you can ensure that all you can construct your trade very well to be successful.

- **Trading Strategies for Scalpers:** Once you have chosen to use scalping to trade the financial market, you must familiarize yourself with the methods, ideas, and techniques required to be successful in the long term. This will ensure that you succeed. There are certain tools required for scalping. Some of them include a direct access broker, five minutes chart and a live news feed and alert. All this is required for trading success.

Your scalping will always begin with preparation and market analysis. Since fundamental news about companies and economics has a bearing on the price, trend, and directions in the market; it will be very important that you get access to a news feed that can provide you with all this information.

Your job is to understand, and trade based on the news, that is news trading. Using fundamental ratios about the stock is also key in making good scalping decisions. These rations help you to figure out new supply and demand forces that will likely breakout after a major event.

But, most of the time, your scalping will heavily be dependent on technical analysis. Using short term historic price information to predict small changes in the market with the help of other technical indications such as moving average, candlestick charts, cups and handles, triangles, and trend channel. Consider volume and price spread before making the trading decisions. Always make sure volume and trend correlated together.

When you are trading with support and resistant indicators, the key is to look for low volatility and a high trading range. Low productivity helps to keep the market calm, avoid light price fluctuation that might work against your trade. Trading range, support and resistance levels will enable us to know where to enter and exit the market to make a profit.

What should be your risk management criteria? Well, you can consider a risk/reward ratio of 1:1. This means you should have a target profit is as equal as the stop loss. You are risking as much as you are earning to make the trade successful because of the price length of the trade.

Examining the trade and focusing on the right market indicators is the key. Unlike position trading, which works better in a bull market, you can execute scalp trades in both bull and bear market.

The strategy in a bear market is to make a profit as prices go upward and the strategy in a bear market is to maximize profits from financial securities that do better in a bad market.

You can use scalp trading for options, stocks, index, futures, and many others. It all depends on your strategy.

Chapter 5.

Day Trading Vs. Swing Trading

Topic Covered:

♦ The Potential Returns of Day Trading Vs. Swing Trading

♦ Capital Needs

♦ Differing of Trading Times

♦ Center, Moment, and Performance

D ay exchanging and swing exchanging each has central focuses and drawbacks. Neither one of them is better than the other. Brokers should pick the one that works best for their aptitudes, tendencies, and way of life. Day trading is increasingly equipped for the people who are individuals who are energetic on full time exchanging.

They are also well equipped with the three Ds, which involve; definitiveness, Demand, and Declaration. These are powerful for beneficial day trading. In order to be accomplished in day trading, it is necessary to have a cognizance of trading and charting. Day trading is a real business. Therefore, representatives should have the choice to stay calm and control their sentiments persevering through an attack.

On the other hand, Swing exchanging is not subjected to the monumental game plan of traits. Anyone with some hypothesis capital can attempt swing trading and it does not require full time thought.

It is an appropriate choice for agents with the need to keep their daily livelihoods, yet also fiddle with the business areas. Swing dealers should moreover have the alternative to apply a mix of critical and examination, rather than specific assessment alone.

The Potential Returns of Day Trading Vs. Swing Trading

In day trading there is the gathering of traders to strengthen the profits quickly. For example: let's say that a trader risks 0.5 percent of their capital on each trade. If they lose, they will be losing 0.5 percent. However, if they succeed, they will earn 1 percent.

On the other hand, let us assume that they win 50 percent of their trades. By any chance that they make 6 trades consistently, they will increase about 1.5 percent in their daily record balance, minus the trading costs.

In about a year, a trading account can grow with more than 200% uncompounded while making as little as 1 percent day by day. On the other hand, while the figures have all the earmarks of being not hard to mimic for tremendous yields, there is nothing straightforward to that extent. It does not always come about; to have twice returns made on victors as compared to the loss in washouts while still having a benefit of 50 percent of the trades you have taken. In day trading, there is a possibility of making a smart increase, while on the other hand, you can quickly make losses.

In swing trading, there is an accumulation of increase and decrease one step at a time than day trading. Currently, you can have some swing trades that achieve huge increases or decreases.

A swing trader can use a comparative risk of 0.5 percent of their capital to make 1 to 2 percent on successful trades. Let us assume that a trader gets 1.5 percent for getting a successful trade while losing 0.5 percent for losing trades. They have 6 trades for each month and succeed in 50 percent of the trades.

Therefore, in a normal month, the swing trader makes 3 percent minus the costs. With consistency, that is 36 percent, which is an amazing figure. These examples show the capability of the two styles of trading.

The ordinary win appears differently concerning typical adversity, or the number of trades will impact a framework's securing potential due to the changing of the degrees of trading won.

If all else fails, day trading has more advantage potential, on any occasion on more diminutive records. As the size of the record creates, it winds up progressively hard to successfully use all the investment on incredibly fleeting day trades.

Capital Needs

Capital necessities waver according to the market that is being traded. The day traders and swing agents can begin with different sizes of investment capital regarding their kind of trade, which can be stocks or forex.

The day trading stocks in the United States require a rate of $25000. There is no genuine least that goes on in swing trade stocks, notwithstanding the way that a swing seller will most likely need in any occasion $10,000 in their record, and in a perfect world have $20000 if they want to gain profits from day trading.

There is legal least that exists today trade. However, it is passed that the sellers start with a capital of $500, whereas in an ideal industry, it needs $1000 or much more. In swing trading, the starting capital approved is about $1500. This size of trading gives you the power to come into any trade at once. In day trading, it can be better where one can start the investment at the rate of $5000 to $7500.

These would, however, depend on the terms of the trading contract. Some agreements would need a huge capital to start, while some may require less such as minimal range contract.

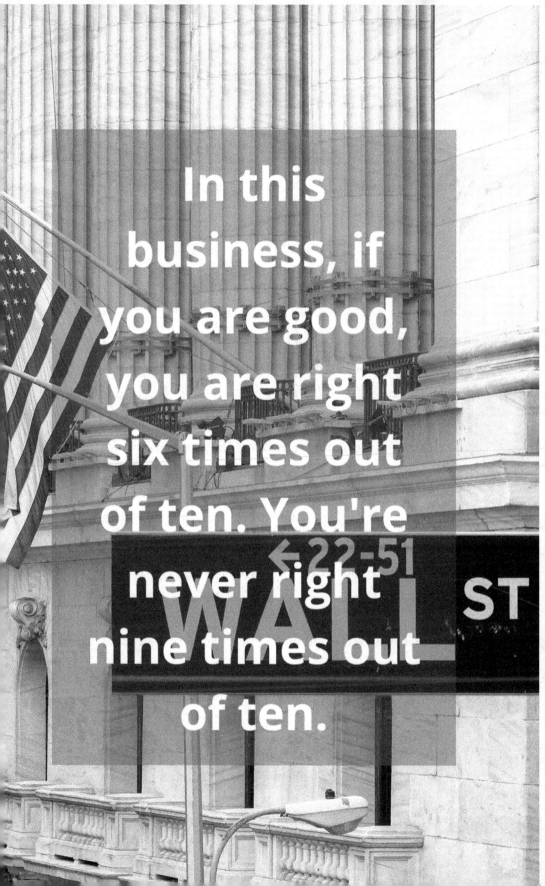

In this business, if you are good, you are right six times out of ten. You're never right nine times out of ten.

In swing trading, several viewing contracts that are necessary for any event is $10000 or $20000 or much more. The amount needed for the whole transactions depends on the important details of the exact agreement being traded.

Differing of Trading Times

Day trading and swing trading require that you, as an investor has time, yet day trading ordinarily possesses generously additional time. Casual financial specialists generally trade for, on any occasion, two hours out of every day. Counting arranging time and blueprint/trading study mean spending on any occasion three to four hours at the PC, in any event. If a casual financial specialist picks to do business for many hours during trading, there is an adventure related to it and it changes to a whole day's work.

On the other hand, swing trading takes up less time. If you are doing swing trading in a regular layout, there is a possibility of finding fresh trades and arrangements on the recent positions each night for 45 minutes. These activities may not be a requirement daily.

Swing traders who engage in trading that last months need to examine for the exchange and update their arrangements every week. This will reduce the time required to spend there to about one hour a day. This is in comparison to the daily consistency. You must engage in day trading when there is an open market. Day trading has a specific timing of the day as compared to swing trading. If you cannot trade during the designated hours, then it would be advisable to take up swing trading, which does not have a limitation of the time. One can trade even if the market has been closed.

The swing traders are not pressured to have second thoughts or to trade too fast. They are relaxed and hang around while monitoring each step, and hence make trades after the market closes, which is always okay. The casual traders make their profits by each second development, so they must be included while the movement happens.

Center, Moment, and Performance

In swing trading and day trading, both need a conventional plan of effort and data to make benefits dependably, despite the way that the learning required doesn't generally book smarts.

Fruitful trading comes about as a result of finding a procedure that conveys an edge, or an advantage over innumerable trades, and a while later executing that strategy over and over. Some data accessible being traded and one productive method can start making payments, nearby bundles and stacks of preparing.

Consistently costs move extraordinarily rather than they did on the last, which means the specialist ought to more likely than not complete his framework within different situations and make adjustments as the situation change.

This displays an irksome test, and dependable results simply start from trying a system that is in different market situations. This will need to make demos account for the trades before the trial because there will be serious speculation. Picking day trading or swing trading narrows to a reason for the character. Day exchanging ordinarily incorporates additional weight, needs upheld fixation designed for widened moment spans and requires fabulous requests. Individuals that have an interest in movement involve speedy reaction, just like PC entertainments and will finally grade toward day trading. Swing trading happens at a more moderate pace, with any more extended sneak's past between exercises compared to going in and out of trades. However, it can regardless be high mass, and most of all, huge demand as well as cleverness.

Swing trading does not require much of your focus; therefore, if you have trouble with focus, this is the trade for you. The quick reaction does not influence swing trading because the trading can happen after the market is closed and the halting of expenses.

In both day and swing trading, there is an offering of leaning that a trader can work for themselves. Merchants regularly wear down their own one of a kind and responsible for financing their records and for all incidents and advantages made. One can battle those swing representatives have a greater open door to the extent time since swing trading possesses minimal time as compared to day trading.

Each of the styles of trading is not better as compared to; they basically suit differentiating needs. Day trading has additional advantage prospective, on any occasion in rate terms on more diminutive assessed platforms of trading. The swing agents contain a prevalent shot of keeping up their rate returns even as their record creates, with a goal in mind.

Capital necessities move an extensive sum over the unusual marketplaces and the methods of trading. In day trading, you require more extra time as compared to swing trading. However, both require adequate preparation to be reliable. If you love change, then day trading is for you. Swing trading, however, is ideal if you require a less stressful option.

The long and short terms of trading mean and show if the trade was started by buying first or selling first. In a long trade, it is started with the interest of selling at a higher profit later.

On the other hand, a short trade is started by selling with the interest of buying again at a lower price to get a benefit.

Chapter 6.

Day Trading Success

Topic Covered:

♦ Common Day Trading Mistakes and How to Avoid Them

♦ Day Trading Tips and Advice

The success of your day trading business depends on a lot of things. If you start on the right foot, you will earn good rewards. The number one secret lies in remaining disciplined and neutral in the sense that your decisions remain independent of your emotions. Doubt, fear, and greed should be the last things on your mind.

As a beginner, you must not allow day to day occurrences to affect you. Although emotional changes are common, they should not influence the way you carry out your trades.

See price movements as something you should adjust towards since these will never be the way you wish them to be. Even when the market assumes a direction that does not favor you, you should not lose focus.

There are several attributes that define successful day traders. These are people who:

- Are ready to risk their money in the trade.

- Manage money in a great way.

- Have confidence in the outcome of each trade.

- Are not afraid to enter and exit positions.

- Are disciplined and patient in their trading.

- Customize very few strategies that work in their favor.

Common Day Trading Mistakes and How to Avoid Them

Quite a few things need to be accomplished before you can celebrate success. Before you engage in the trade, here are some of the mistakes you need to beware of and to avoid:

- **Adding More Capital to a Trade That Is Going Down:** New traders always get tempted to average positions down when the price is on the decline with the hope that things will get better. This is one of the worst mistakes that you can do. The market prices may decline further, resulting in exponential loss. Instead of doing this, set stop orders early into the trade and close positions as soon as things become bad.

- **Continuing to Trade Even after Losing Consecutively:** When day trading, there are two figures you always need to have at the back of your mind. The risk/ reward rate, as well as the win rate. The win rate is often represented as a percentage. For instance, if you win 30 out of 50 trades, your rate of winning is 60%. Successful traders are those who can maintain at least 50% or more as the win rate. The risk/ reward ratio refers to the amount you win as compared to the amount you lose in each trade. For instance, if your winning trades cost $80 and the losing trades are $40 then the reward/ risk ratio becomes $80/$40, which is 2. To be considered successful, this ratio should always be at least 1.

- **Not Setting Stop Loss Parameters:** Not setting stop-loss orders in your trade will always lead to danger. The work of stop-loss orders is to limit the amount of capital you lose when market prices deflate against you. They moderate losses on your behalf.

- **Working with the Wrong Broker:** Trusting a broker with your capital is one of the best ways you can grow your day trading business. However, if you choose a broker that does not understand how to manage your cash, you will end up losing most of your fortune. You also need to understand how much commission the broker will charge in advance and if there are any hidden charges associated with the partnership. Beware of scammers who also parade themselves as brokers. These can lure you into investing in non-existent platforms.

- **Taking Several Related Trades:** As you start day trading, you may get excited at the many opportunities available on the trading platforms. This can lead you into opening multiple positions at the same time. You may end up getting these positions from the same stocks and this can become risky if the stock does not perform well on the market. When day trading, diversification is key. It protects you from losing too much on one type of stock. However, as a new trader, you need to be watchful of the number of trades you open in a day. You may be tempted to make multiple trades as a way of minimizing the risk of loss. But this is not a good idea if you are not quite conversant with the market.

- **Investing What You Are Not Ready to Lose:** If you are not comfortable losing the amount of cash you are investing in day trading, simply do not do it. Most day traders get into the business without defining how much they are ready to lose. After they have lost the cash, they get frustrated. You should only risk 1 percent of your capital on each trade by setting your stop-loss orders correctly. When you do this, only a small percentage of your cash will be lost at the end of the day, however much you trade.

As much as you would have set your loss limits, it is essential that you try to manage any ongoing losses and maintain them at a minimum low.

If you keep losing at most 1 percent on each trade, you would have to part with a huge percentage of your capital at the end of each trading period. The fact that you have defined the loss limits does not necessarily mean that you must lose this amount.

- **Entering the Trade Blindly:** There are new traders who ignore their strategies completely, getting into the trade with no plan. This occurs partly when an individual keeps gaining on several trades in a row. When this happens, you can become overconfident that you cannot lose a trade. This confidence can make you invest everything you have, and this can lead to tremendous losses.

- **Not Carrying out an Analysis of the Market:** Once you have made several successful trades, you may start trading without analyzing the necessary market and financial data. It gets dangerous when you get into the market without understanding how the prices will change in future. Although long-term fundamental analysis is unnecessary for day traders, you need to understand this information for your future trades.

- **Not Having a Plan:** This is one of the biggest mistake day traders do. A trading plan often outlines the strategies and activities you need to engage in during the trade. It handles the when and how parts of day trading. When you do not have a plan, you may keep entering and exiting positions without any guidelines. Doing this will leave you unsure of what to expect from the trading period. Not having a plan also means that you are unable to estimate the risks involved in each trade you engage in.

- **Predicting News Before it Comes Out:** Some traders get to know of upcoming news and act on it even before it is released to the public. This looks like staying ahead of the market, but it is not. It is not advisable that you take positions before any news item gets confirmed. The stock price may move in either direction or this direction may change too fast. You need to understand this and trade basing on the current market trend, not unconfirmed news.

Day Trading Tips and Advice

As you begin day trading, there are several methods you can use to ensure you increase your chances of making profit. Some of these include the inside bar strategy, gapping up and down as well as the use of Fibonacci patterns.

The Inside bar Breakout Strategy

This is a strategy that utilizes two bars to assist you in day trading. One bar is always smaller than the other. The first bar is known as the mother bar, while the other bar is the inside bar.

The bar is used in day trading to identify the trend's direction. When you trade this way, the process is called breakout playing. The intention is always to place stop orders for buying or selling either at the top or bottom of the mother bar.

These orders are then filled when the price goes beyond the bar edges. If the mother bar is relatively large, the stop orders can be placed in the middle of the bar.

Gapping Up and Gapping Down

Gaps refer to price breaks often displayed in stock charts. These gaps always occur when there is a sudden release in a news item that impacts the price of stocks. The announcement may be about a new product release, mergers and acquisition or wars. These are always influential enough on the price of stocks.

Gaps are always represented on the charts as a blank space between bars. Gaps offer great signals that help you determine whether to purchase or you're your trades. When there is a gap down, this is the right time to sell your positions. When there is a gap up, it is the right time to purchase stock. When a price gap occurs, you may spend a few minutes studying the market range before you can decide what to do with your positions. Generally, there are four primary gap types:

- **Full gap up**—this is a gap created when the day's opening price for a certain stock is higher than the highest price attained by stock the previous day.

- **Partial gap up**—this is when the current opening price is below the stocks lowest price for the previous day.

- **Full gap down**—this is created when the day's opening price is lower than the lowest price attained by a stock the previous day.

- **Partial gap down**—this is when the current opening price is lower than the previous day's closing price but higher than the day's lowest price.

Besides sudden news items, gaps can also result from certain technical and fundamental factors.

For instance, if the earnings received by a certain organization are more than the anticipated amount, the price of the stocks related to the company may change drastically by the following day.

This implies that the opening cost will be much higher than the previous day's closing amount.

Chapter 7.

Trading Platforms

Topic Covered:

♦ MetaTrader 4/5 (MT4/5)

♦ Ninja Trader and cTrader

♦ ProRealTime, Installing the Trading Platform

D ay traders have a variety of trading platforms to choose from. A trading platform is a program or software that a trader uses to access market data, conduct their analysis, and place trades. There are tens of available platforms in the market. Recently, due to the growth of the trading industry, more options have been introduced, and competition has become stiff.

At the end of the day, it is up to the trader to decide on the platform or platforms to use.

MetaTrader 4 (MT4)

MT4 is one of the oldest trading platforms in the industry. It is one of the programs that led to the growth of retail traders as it enabled them to access the market. Traders find it highly reliable and easy to use, making it the most popular trading platform in use for decades now.

- It is highly stable.
- It supports a lot of indicators, trading instruments, and robots.
- It can work on all mobile and computer operating systems.
- It is available in almost all brokerage companies.
- It is free.

MetaTrader 5 (MT5)

Just like the names suggest, MT4 and MT5 are related since they are made by the same company (Metaquotes). Their major difference is that the MT5 platform is more advanced and includes more features than the MT4. For instance, the MT5 is even more stable. It is faster, holds more robots and indicators, and comes with more trading instruments.

It is advisable that even if you start out with MT4, you should gradually transition to MT5 as the older platform may stop being used in the future. We are going to base our learning on this newer trading platform. You can also use the MT4 as they operate the same way.

Ninja Trader

The Ninja Trader platform is quite young compared to the MT4. It came into the market in 2004. All the same, some traders prefer it over the MT4. While the MT4 is mostly suitable for trading currencies (forex and cryptocurrency), the Ninja Trader readily supports forex, stock, and futures trading.

In addition to this, the platform offers trade simulation, automated strategy development, and advanced charting tools and abilities.

Some disadvantages of the Ninja Trader that keep the MT4 in the lead include:

- Users must buy a license or lease the platform to be able to execute trades, and plug-ins like indicators and robots are not free.

- It is not a market data provider, so traders must connect to a data provider like Kinetick or Google.

cTrader

The cTrader software comes third after the Metaquotes platforms and Ninja Trader. It has been displaying stiff competition in recent years, and many brokers have been taking it up. Some of the features that make it highly competitive include fast trade execution, cheaper costs of trades, vast device support, and advanced charting capabilities.

However, unlike the other platforms, it does not support Windows Phone OS.

ProRealTime

ProRealTime is a web-based platform (it does not need to be installed on a computer) as it is backed up on the cloud network of the company. It uses a unique coding language (ProRealCode) to create market analyzing tools.

While this feature makes it unique, it also means there are fewer tools available online. Another disadvantage is that users must pay to use the platform and access real-time data.

ESignal

ESignal might not be the most popular trading platform, but it is a favorite tool for advanced traders who prefer to customize their own trading approaches. Once a trader learns the supported coding language, they can create their own indicators, trading strategies, and other analytic tools. In addition, eSignal allows a trader to view over 500 trading instruments at a go. On the downside, traders must pay annual or monthly fees to gain access to market feed. Second, the platform is not common in most brokerage companies. Remember, it is up to you as the trader to decide on the type of trading platform to use.

Though, the MT5 is user-friendly and contains all the necessary tools, instruments, and features that a trader needed.

Installing the Trading Platform

The trading platforms are available on the brokers' websites. You need to sign up with a broker of your choice before accessing any trading platform. Once registered, the broker will provide you with a list of all the trading platforms that they support for you to choose from.

The installation process is quite simple and usually requires filling in some personal details and other information that will be provided by the broker. In our case, we shall be using the MT5, which is very similar to the MT4 platform.

The MT5 is very easy to install. To make it even better, we can use the platform for learning purposes without signing up with any broker. However, this will only be a demo account. To access the MT5, head over to the Metaquotes website, and download the MT5.

I recommend this method because you will not have to undergo the long process of applying for an account. You can do this when you are ready to use a live account. Once you have downloaded the MT5 file to your computer, run it and make sure your internet is active.

Types of Charts on MT5

Now that you have the trading platform ready let us look at the types of charts that you can use. The four windows with a lot of graphics that you can see above are known as charts. Let us look at the three types of charts that we can use for analyzing the market:

- **Line Chart:** To activate a line chart, you need to first select one of the charts in the open windows. Once you have chosen your chart, click on the "Line chart" icon at the top of your MT5.

This is a simple graphic that represents the movement of prices. When it is sloping upward, it means the price was increasing, and when it slopes downward, it means the price was decreasing.

- **Bar Chart:** To activate a bar chart, you need to click on the "Bar chart" tool at the top of your MT5. Unlike a line chart, the bar chart has more details. It shows the opening and closing of prices.

The vertical lines with tiny horizontal lines on either side are called "hashes."

The hashes on the left show the opening prices, while those on the right show the closing prices.

The top of the bars represents the highest point that price went, while the bottom part shows the lowest point that price touched. Bar charts are also known as OHLC charts where 'O' stands for the opening price, 'H' for the highest point that price went, 'L' for the lowest point, and 'C' for the closing price of the bar.

- **Candlestick Charts:** Candlestick charts are the most interesting charts. They use bars that look like candles with wicks to show the performance of price. Just like bar charts, they also show the open and closing prices, as well as the highs and lows of prices. However, they look different in that they have wider bodies and single lines on either side called 'wicks.' Candlestick bars are also colored to represent prices going up or down within a selected timeframe.

To activate a candlestick bar, click the "candlesticks" icon next to where you found the line and bar chart icons.

You can customize the colors of the candles as you wish. In most cases, bearish candles are filled with red color, while bullish ones are filled with green. However, the colors have no effect on one's trading; they only help one to see price behavior more clearly.

Chapter 8.

Fundamental Analysis

Topic Covered:

- Determine the stock or security
- Economic forecast
- Company Analysis
- Business model

- Competitive advantage
- Management
- Market share
- Industry growth

The main purpose of fundamental analysis is to receive a forecast and thereby profit from future price movements. There are certain questions that fundamental analysis seeks to answer:

- Is the firm's revenue growing?
- Is it profitable in both the short and long terms?
- Can I afford to settle its liabilities?
- Can it outsmart its competitors?
- Is the company's outlook genuine or fraudulent?

These are just a few examples of the numerous questions that fundamental analysis seeks to answer. Sometimes traders also want answers to questions not mentioned above.

In short, therefore, the purpose is to obtain and profit from expected price movements in the short-to-near-term future. Most of the fundamental analysis is conducted at the company level because traders and investors are mostly interested in information that will enable them to make a decision at the markets.

They want information that will guide them in selecting the most suitable stocks to trade at the markets. As such, traders and investors searching for stocks to trade will resort to examining the competition, a company's business concept, its management, and financial data.

For a proper forecast regarding future stock prices, a trader is required to take into consideration a company's analysis, industry analysis, and even the overall economic outlook.

This way, a trader will be able to determine the latest stock price as well as predicted future stock price. When the outcome of fundamental analysis is not equal to the current market price, then it means that the stock is overpriced or perhaps even undervalued.

There is no clear-cut pathway or method of conducting the fundamental analysis. However, we can break down the entire process so that you know exactly where to begin. The most preferred approach is the top-down approach. We begin by examining the general economy followed by industry group before finally ending with the company in question. In some instances, though, the bottom-up approach is also used.

Determine the Stock or Security

You need to first have a stock or security in mind. There are many factors that determine the stocks to trade. For instance, you may want to target blue-chip companies noted for exemplary stock market performance, profitability, and stability. You also want to focus on companies that constitute one of the major indices such as the Dow Jones Industrial Average or S&P 500. The stocks should have large trading volumes for purposes of liquidity.

Economic Forecast

The overall performance of the economy basically affects all companies. Therefore, when the economy fares well, then it follows that most companies will succeed. This is because the economy is like a tide while the various companies are vessels directed by the tide.

There is a general correlation between the performance of companies and their stocks and the performance of the general economy. The economy can also be narrowed to focus on specific sectors.

For instance, we have the energy sector, transport sector, manufacturing, hospitality, and so on. Narrowing down to specific sectors is crucial for proper analysis. There are certain factors that we need to consider when looking at the general economy. We have the market size, growth rate, and so on. Basically, when stocks move in the markets, they tend to move as a group. This is because when a sector does well, then most companies in that sector will also excel.

Company Analysis

One of the most crucial steps in fundamental analysis is company analysis. At this stage, you will come up with a compiled shortlist of companies. Different companies have varying capabilities and resources.

The aim, in our case, is to find companies that can develop and keep a competitive advantage over its competitors and others in the same market. Some of the factors to look for are financial records, a solid management team, and a credible business plan.

When it comes to companies, the best approach is to check out a company's qualitative aspects, followed by quantitative before checking out its financial outlook.

We shall begin with the qualitative aspect of the company analysis. One of the most crucial is the company's business model.

Business Model

One of the most crucial questions that analysts and all others ask about a company is exactly what it does. This is a simple yet fundamental question. A company's business model is simply what the company does to make money. The best way to learn about a company's business model is to visit its website and learn more about what it does. You can also check out its 10-K filings to find out more.

Competitive Advantage

We also need to take a closer look at a company's competitive advantage. Any company that is to survive the long term needs to have a competitive edge over its competitors. A company with one such advantage must be Coca Cola because of the unique nature of its products. Others are Microsoft, Toyota, and Google.

Their business models provide them with a competitive edge that is hard for others to compete with. In general, a unique competitive edge is where a company has clear trade-offs and options for customers compared to competitors, a unique product or service, reliable operational effectiveness, and a great fit in all activities.

Management

Also crucial for any serious company is its management. Any company worth its salt must have top quality management in major positions. Investors and analysts usually look at the level and quality of management to determine their competences, experience, strengths, and capabilities.

This is because they hold in their hands the fate of a company. Even a great company with excellent ideas and plans can fail if the management is not right. It is advisable to find out how qualified, experienced, successful, and committed the leadership of a company is. For instance, do they have prior experience at senior levels? Is there a track record and can management deliver on its stated objectives? These are crucial questions that should be answered appropriately for a positive conclusion.

Industry Factors

When conducting your company analysis, there are other factors that you will need to consider here. These factors include business cycles, competition, growth in the industry, government regulation, and others. It is advisable to also have an understanding of the workings of a specific industry that you are interested in.

Government Policy

In countries such as the United States, government policy is extremely crucial. When conducting fundamental analysis, you really should take this into perspective because certain policies can completely kill an industry.

Market Share

Different companies within the same industry sometimes must work hard to gain market share. There are sometimes a lot of companies fighting for a small share of customers, especially at a local level. If a company controls about 85% of the market, then it means it is a solid company with strong fundamentals. A strong market share also means that a company possesses that competitive edge over its customers. It also means that the company is larger than its rivals and hence has a great outlook.

Industry Growth

This is also another aspect that should be taken into account. Some companies may have everything else working for them, but future growth prospects may not be so bright. It is important to assess an industry and confirm whether there are any prospects for future growth

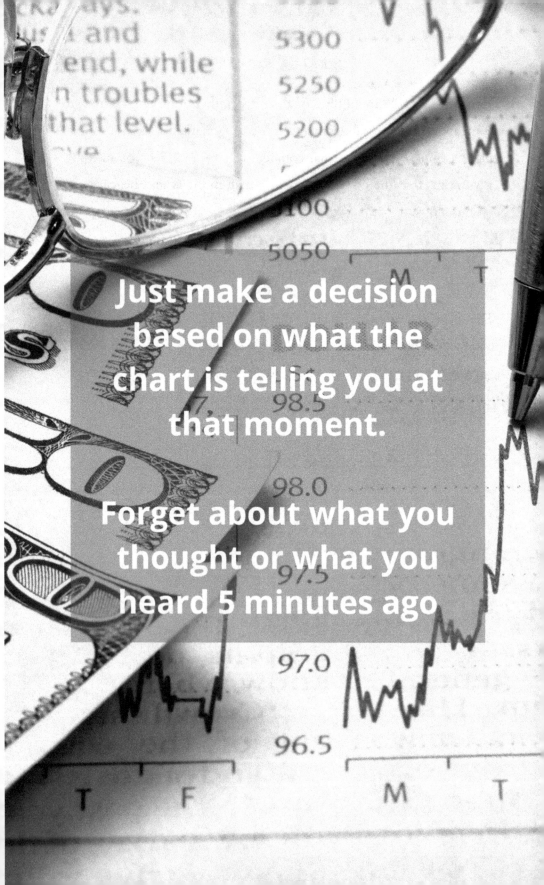

Just make a decision based on what the chart is telling you at that moment.

Forget about what you thought or what you heard 5 minutes ago

Chapter 9.

Paper Trading

Topic Covered:

♦ Learning to Trade with Zero Risks

♦ No Stress Involved

♦ Build Your Confidence

♦ You Can Make Mistakes

♦ Test Strategies That Work

Before concluding that day trading is challenging for you, you need to understand how it works. Novice traders are often advised to engage in paper trading before anything else. Paper trading refers to a process whereby traders are given the opportunity of trading without using their actual money.

In other words, they get to trade by using virtual money provided by their brokers. Since there is no real money involved during paper trading, this gives any trader the opportunity of testing their strategies.

If you will be making profits while using paper trading, then there is a good chance that you will also make profits once you begin using your money.

Also, a trader can easily make relevant adjustments to their trading strategies to make certain that they make profits from time to time. Since you will not be using real money to trade, you must be wondering why it is important for you to engage in paper trading. Paper trading is a fundamental step in your trading experience. It helps you to learn the basics of online trading without putting your money on the line.

Therefore, you get to test different trading strategies, whether they could work or not. Some of the importance of paper trading you should be aware of is detailed as follows. There is no reason why you should hesitate to paper trade since there are numerous paper trading platforms for you to choose from.

This means that it would be relatively easy for you to practice trading. You should do some digging to find out the best paper trading platforms that suit you. A good way of evaluating them is by checking the cool features which are provided. For instance, a feature you should not miss in the platform you use is a tool that will show you how you are performing as compared to other traders.

Learning to Trade with Zero Risks

Essentially, one of the main reasons why you should make good use of paper trading platforms is that they help you learn how to trade with zero risks involved. Consequently, you get to develop some sense of confidence in day trading. One huge mental roadblock faced by most traders is the fear of losing their investments.

This prevents most traders from trying to trade. With paper trading, this cannot happen. You will not lose any money. In fact, you will be benefiting from the learning experience you will gain.

No Stress Involved

Traders will have to deal with stress from time to time. When their investments are not performing well, this could have a psychological effect on them.

A trader who incurs huge losses consecutively could give up in the process. When one chooses to engage in paper trading, they will be preventing themselves from having to deal with stress. You are new to the trading industry. As such, the last thing you need is some negative vibe proving to you that you cannot be successful in day trading.

So, start using a paper trading account to relieve yourself from stress, which comes about when traders make trading mistakes.

Build Your Confidence

The confidence you gain in using paper trading accounts is invaluable. At first, you will approach the world of online trading with uncertainty. Well, cut yourself some slack. There is nothing much you know about trading in stocks, forex, and options. As a matter of fact, there are certain terms which could confuse you and you might fail to take advantage of market opportunities when they present themselves.

Using paper trading accounts helps you to build confidence as you begin day trading. The assumption that your account is literally growing will motivate you to continue learning. Your focus will be on learning more with the hopes of earning real money soon.

You Can Make Mistakes

There is no way you will learn how to trade without making mistakes. In order to become a skillful trader, you must know the common mistakes which most traders make. In every mistake you make while paper trading, you will be better placed to make the right moves once you use real money.

Undeniably, you cannot make the same mistake twice. If a move generates losses, you will try your best to avoid it in your next purchases. Also, you might make mistakes while selling your securities.

For instance, you could sell too early or late, which could affect your financial position. The ability to make mistakes while using a paper trading account makes it essential for any beginner to use it.

Test Strategies That Work

Testing strategies when you begin trading will only increase your risks. You will run the risk of losing your capital as there are chances that you could make mistakes here and there.

Concerning this issue, you need to use a paper trading account to put your strategies to the test. You can test as many strategies as you can. Your main point should be to find one strategy you can implement once you begin trading with real money.

Keeping this in mind, new traders should not be afraid of failing. They should not be concerned about making mistakes while paper trading. Honestly, they should make as many mistakes as possible to warrant that they are well exposed to the market trends.

Paper trading could be an excellent platform for novice traders to learn the art of trading. The best part is that they get to experiment without using real money. This infers that there is nothing to lose when using paper trading accounts.

You will only lose out on gaining the right trading experience if you choose not to use a paper trading account. Traders should always remember to use the same brokers for their real accounts. Why is this important?

Well, using the same broker gives you the confidence that you are not far enough from reality. Consequently, it is vital that you compare options before settling for any broker in the market.

There are several points you need to keep in mind to ensure you make the most out of day trading.

Get Acquainted

Before rushing to trade virtually, you should take steps to familiarize yourself with the platform you will be using. Get to know the common terms which are using in day trading. You don't want to incur losses just because of silly mistakes you ought to have avoided right from the get-go.

Take Notes

When trading virtually, remember that you are doing this to learn how to trade online. Therefore, it makes a lot of sense that you should take notes. Record anything you think it is important. If there is something that you did not understand, don't move to the next step without clarifying everything. After the markets close, give yourself some time to go over what you learned.

Execute Bad Trades

Don't just trade on good markets. If possible, try and make the wrong decisions and see what happens. The importance of using paper accounts is for you to learn more about the possible mistakes you could make while day trading. Therefore, don't focus on doing everything right. Execute bad trades and learn from them.

Analyze in Sets

The best way of evaluating your performance is by carrying out your analysis in sets. Group your trades in different sets of 10, 20, or 50 and make your evaluation. Doing this helps you know which trades performed well. Accordingly, from the trading strategies which you will be adopting, you will determine the best ones to adopt.

Euphoria Trading

A big risk involved in paper trading is that a trader might be lured to make certain moves that they wouldn't make in ordinary cases. When they are making huge losses, they might also fail to take their mistakes seriously since there is no money involved in the trading process. This means that a trader might fail to respond in the same manner that they would have done when using real money.

Delayed Data

Traders might fail to gain the real-time data experience that they would have had when using paid accounts. Therefore, delayed data could negatively affect their trading experience. Sadly, there are unscrupulous brokers who might display fake date to their clients. A trader could end up getting the wrong impression about their day trading performance. Overall, it is imperative to use paper trading, bearing in mind that there are many benefits associated with it. There are many signs that could indicate you are a skilled trader. Nonetheless, the best way of knowing that you are surely on the right path is by educating yourself. This makes it vital for you to use a paper trading account.

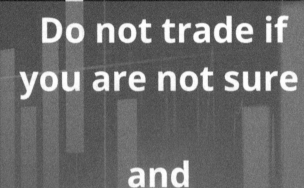

Do not trade if you are not sure

and

Do not increase any losing position.

Chapter 10.

Order Types

Topic Covered:

♦ Market Order

♦ Limit Order

♦ Buy-Stop Order

♦ Managing your position

You need to understand the difference between different order types, including market orders, limit orders, and buy-stop orders, to place the right order.

Market Order

Simply tell your broker to buy shares at the best available price. If you choose to buy or sell using market orders, then you let the market, which is automated computers, fill your order using the best national bid and offer price (NBBO). This means your broker must ensure that you receive the best available bid and ask price. Unfortunately, you may get a very bad fill during certain market conditions, like a fast market, if you use a market order. In fact, one of the only reasons you would choose a market order is to have an immediate fill, but you may not get the most competitive price.

A market order is a disaster. For example: your sell order may be filled 10, 15, or 20 lowers than you anticipated during a very fast market or flash crash. Although a flash crash is a relatively rare occurrence, remember that when placing a market order, you give the market full control over your order, and that's never the wisest move.

Buy Example: Microsoft trades $23.82 (bid) to $23.83(ask). You enter a buy market order and your order will be completed at $23.83 in seconds.

Sell Example: Microsoft's $23.82 $23.83 trading. You enter a selling market order, and seconds later, your order is $23.82.

Another market order problem is slippage (the difference between the estimated market price and the actual price you bought or sold).

Occasionally, slippage is expected to reduce your profits. Day traders rarely use market orders for all the above reasons, and instead, use limit orders.

Limit Order

The maximum price you're willing to pay or the minimum price you're willing to sell when you enter a limit order. Your order is completed when the stock reaches the price you specify. When purchasing, your limit order is lower than the current asking price. When selling, your limit order is higher than the current bid price.

Basically, you instruct the brokerage to buy at or above the specified price. You're setting parameters. Know this: the stock may be trading close to $23, but if you want to bid $22,50 you can. The order will be filled immediately, but you can enter a limit order at any price.

While limits are the preferred method of buying or selling stock, they have a downside. For example, if the stock never reaches the limit price, your order will not be filled. You'll be dropping nowhere to go unless you re-enter your price.

Buy Example: Microsoft is trading $23.83 asking price, the price you must pay if you want to buy it right now. You set a $23.50 limit order, ensuring you won't pay more than $23.50 to buy this stock. If Microsoft drops to $23.50 or less, the order is filled. However, if the stock never drops to $23.50, the order isn't triggered, you didn't buy the shares, and no harm is done.

Sell Example: Microsoft trades at a $23.82 bid price, the price you'll get if you want to sell it right now. You set a $24 limit order. If Microsoft reaches $24 or higher, your order is completed. If the stock doesn't reach $24, the order isn't completed.

If you want to be filled in immediately, you can place an order that is higher than or lower than the current bid price. In other words, if the current stock request is $23.83 per share and you want to buy immediately, you can enter $23.84. You'll be filled immediately, and probably at $23.83.

If the current bid price is $23.82 and you want to sell immediately, you can enter a $23.81 price. You'll probably be filled in a second.

Buy-Stop Order

Another convenient type is buy-stop. Let's say you don't want to miss out if a stock suddenly moves higher (like a bullish chart pattern). By entering a buy-stop, you tell the brokerage to enter an order to buy the stock at a higher price. Once that price is reached, your order becomes a buying market order.

Example buy-stop order: Microsoft is trading $23.82 at $23.83. In a $24 buy-stop order. If the stock hits $24, it becomes a market order. Once the order is triggered at $24 (or higher) buy-stop price, it is filled at the next available price. However, if the stock does not hit $24 (or higher), the order will remain unfulfilled.

You can also use this order to buy a stock at a higher price, but you're away from your computer and can't enter it manually. You may have to leave the house and don't want to miss out if the stock keeps rising. Then you could order a buy-stop. The only danger with this order is if, for example, the stock suddenly gaps at the open market. You could get filled much higher than you expected.

Therefore, when making the trade, use the buy-stop order, and avoid using this order type on the open market. Another solution is a buy-stop limit order.

Example of a $23.83 buy-stop limit order: Microsoft currently trades $23.82. You enter a $24 buy-stop limit. If Microsoft hits $24, it turns into a limit order, buying the shares at $24 or better. If after the trigger the stock doesn't drop below $24, your order will remain open.

Also, it's possible for the market to blast through your buy order without filling. Bottom line: since these orders are so flexible, it's suggested that you first experiment with them to determine which one meets your needs.

Note: You can also enter two prices with a buy-stop limit order. First, the stop price, the trigger. Second, the limit price is the most you're willing to pay for the stock. Check with your brokerage to learn their rules.

Managing your position

Managing position size is one of the keys to your trader's success and an essential aspect of risk management. This means adjusting your share position size, so you don't risk too much money if you're wrong. For example, some rookies always buy 1,000 shares regardless of stock price or how much money they have in their accounts.

It's a huge mistake. Proper share size depends on many factors, including stop-losses.

Chapter 11.

Becoming an Established Day Trader

Topic Covered:

♦ Adapt to Flourish

♦ Wait for It

♦ Use Self Discipline

♦ Past Experiences as Lessons

♦ Pocket that Cash

After you have learned all the steps to go through getting started with day trading and the different processes that are associated with it, you should be able to easily become an established day trader. This doesn't necessarily mean that you will be as good as the people who have been doing it for years, but it does mean that you will be able to work toward making a career out of it.

It is not uncommon for people who are working in the day trading field to completely replace their full-time income and to become someone who works for themselves and makes a fortune while doing so.

Financial freedom and stability are both possible once you have established yourself as a day trader and once you have made the decision to stick to it in a way that allows you to be as successful as possible.

There are many different options that come along with day trading and making money is nearly always the result of following the right path toward success with day trading.

If you follow these ideas, you will be able to gain financial freedom as a day trader and become among the best people who trade.

Adapt to Flourish

There will be times when you must adapt while you are day trading. There may be things that you are not accustomed to, and there may even be things that you have never seen before. Be prepared for this and make sure that you can handle it.

If you are prepared to adapt to everything that is going on with your day trading, you will know the right way to handle it and everything that needs to come along with day trading. There are many different options, and if you don't know the right way to do it, you may find that you are failing as a day trader.

That is something you will not want after you have already established yourself as a trader. Some things that can happen is that there may be unexpected huge fluctuations in prices, there may be problems with the system, and you may lose out on some of the stocks that you wanted.

Don't let any of these things get in your way and don't let them bring you down. Just be prepared for them, and there will be no way that they can disrupt your day trading strategies.

If you can adapt, you will be great at day trading. You should make sure that you are always prepared for different things and that you don't have to worry about the problems that come along with trading.

Day trading is all about being prepared to jump when you need to and that is one of the biggest problems that traditional investors have when it comes to day trading. They are used to having the chance to be able to take their time and figure out what they are doing.

Wait for It

Patience is huge when it comes to day trading. You may find that you have three or four days where you are not able to buy any quality stocks or make any investment.

This is something that can be expected and something that you must be prepared for when you are day trading. The positive part of that is that when you have waited for a period to be able to get the trades that you want, you will be able to benefit from the trades that are much better than the ones that you passed up.

Having patience is important in any trading but is especially important in day trading. If you do not have patience and simply buy whatever stocks you want, even if you think that they are not going to do well, you may end up with stocks that you cannot get rid of at the end of the day.

The point of day trading is to start the next day with no stocks and nothing going on so that you can get a clean slate each time that you start your day.

Waiting for the right opportunity is a way for you to be able to get more out of day trading. It is something that you must be prepared to do and something that can be hard for some people – especially those who are used to not having to wait for anything.

You need to make sure that you are trying y our hardest and that you are going to be able to enjoy the benefits that come along with day trading. If you don't have patience, you won't be able to enjoy any of the about because you will never be able to make a truly good deal.

Use Self Discipline

Having discipline can sometimes be hard when you are trying to make money. You may be tempted by the great stocks that you find even if you think that they are not a good price. This is something that can be detrimental to your career in day trading, though, because if you spend too much money on stocks and then lose all of that money, you won't have the chance to be able to invest more money and be able to make that money.

If you are disciplined with the money that you have, you will be able to save more of it. This means that you can put more money back to be able to invest in higher quality stocks and other investments.

It also means that you will be safer if something happens to your trading and the money that you have. Just always be sure that you are going to be able to save money and that the discipline that you are doing is not something that is going to be detrimental.

By not having too much self-discipline, you are going to allow yourself to have the best chance possible. When you are day trading, it can be easy to get caught up and save too much money. This just means that you are keeping too much of it to yourself and not making the investments that you should be to be able to make a lot of money.

There is a delicate balance that lies between being self-disciplined and having too much self-discipline. Try to find that balance, keep it in your sights, and always practice it so that you will be able to truly enjoy the process of day trading. It is not fun and there is no point in doing it if you are never able to make any actual money from it.

Past Experiences as Lessons

It is always a good idea to track your trades when you are first getting started, but it can also be beneficial when you are an experienced day trader, too.

When you can make sure that you are working as a trader, you will benefit from understanding everything that you need to be able to get the most out of your trades. You can use these experiences that you had in the beginning as lessons later in your trading career.

It may seem like it is impossible for you to be able to get the most out of trading if you don't have anything to help you remember, but it is a good idea to try to remember this information.

Keeping a log will help you remember what you did in the past that worked and what you did in the past that did not work. Understanding each of these things can make it easier for you later.

If you can keep track of what you spent, how much you invested and all the options that were included with your spending on different things, you will have a better chance of working toward your goals.

The biggest aspect of trading is learning from your past experiencing. Figure out what worked for you, what didn't, and what you can do in the future to make things even better for yourself.

There are so many different options when it comes to trading, so be sure that you keep track of these and of the options that are included.

Write them down and keep them close so that you will always be able to reference them while you are trading.

Pocket that Cash

While you are trading, you should invest some of the profits that you make back into trading. This is the only way that you will grow in your business, and you will be able to improve your business in this way. If you are going to continue to do that, set aside a certain amount of profit to be able to invest back into trading.

This is the easiest way for you to figure out how much you need to spend and how much you can afford to put back into your pocket. It may take some time, but you will eventually be profiting above the set amount that you wanted to be able to put back into the business.

You should work hard to be able to include all the different options that are with your trading business and to be able to get the most out of the trading experience. Try to pocket as much as you can after you have put it back. This can go toward your income.

The more that your pocket, the easier it will be for you to replace a full-time job with day trading. You will eventually get so good at day trading that you won't have to worry about working.

This will be your income. You may even find that you are making more as a day trader and that you don't have to worry about everything that comes along with having a "real" job. Pocketing your money as much as possible is the first step to building your fortune with day trading and giving yourself the financial freedom to live life the way that you want to.

Conclusion

By now, you should have a good understanding of day trading and the different financial markets that you can trade. Hopefully, the lessons you have learned in this beginner's guide will help you to decide if this is really a good career for you.

Day trading is quite different and difficult from other trading styles, due to the short time frame for making decisions related to entry and exit points. The basic investing rule for intraday trading is don't trust what you think, trust what you see. Understanding the basics of day trading and experiment with those basics with the help of demo accounts could help intraday traders to make big gains.

Intraday trading also involves several trading strategies and indicators to maximize returns and reduce losses. If you don't have a strong command on the technical side, the risk of losing the trade is higher.

One of the key things that we have taught you in this is that you need to exercise the art of patience. Being patient with the market, the plans, the people, and your marketing and decision making is going to let you have more power financially and more power in this field. You need to make sure that you have the patience to be able to push through and reach your goals. This takes time and work, and if you have the patience, you will be able to do this successfully.

Remembering that this is a hot commodity today will serve you well as well. When you realize how many people are in this field and how many people are wanting to do the same thing and have a great level of success like you are is going to help you.

Going into day trading is a big step and should not be taken lightly. With too little prep, you may find that you lose your money in your account. Nobody wants to be that person who never got off the ground, so take this seriously and continue to educate yourself.

Day trading can be a very lucrative career if done in the proper way, with planning and strategy. Be that person. Plan your heart out, and you will see the results in your turnarounds.

Take the time to explore different platforms and get to know which one you would prefer. Decide what kind of trader you want to be, full-time, part-time, and the like. When it comes to day trading, you can't have too much information going into it.

Protect yourself, and make sure you understand what you are planning to do. Trust me, you will come out on the other side a whole lot more appreciative of the information. When you see the positive money coming in, you will begin to see research as a helper and not as a nuisance.

When it comes to going from a novice day trader to an expert and master of the market, it is important to approach the task with the appropriate mindset for true success.

This means that you will need to anticipate that it will take some time for everything to properly click into place and that it is perfectly normal to have a rocky few weeks when you find your trade footing. If you perfect the trading plan for you and keep at it, however, eventually things should right themselves and you should see your profits start to move in the opposite direction.

Regardless of what steps you take, and how carefully you go about mitigating all the risks that you run across, it is also important to understand that there is some risk you will never be able to get rid of completely, nor would you want to.

While sometimes this risk means that an otherwise surefire trade isn't going to work out the way you planned, if there was no risk, then there could be no reward as prices would always proceed as planned and profits would remain uniform and uninspired. Instead of shying away from risk at all its levels, it is best that you embrace it for what it is, a tool that can be brought to the forefront as needed with clear expectations as to what use it will be and what results it will produce overall.

The markets never move in a straight line nor are they always consolidating and trending. Day traders also must manage distinctive kinds of unpredictability and uncertainties. Therefore, day traders should also know how to trade in a volatile environment, and they should also understand how they can use different indicators to manage the volatility.

Day traders should always know about different trends, breakouts, and sideways trading if they want to succeed in day trading. Analyzing charts and predicting trends could become easier for day traders if they do some training before trading with real cash.

Dave R. W. Graham

A Gift for You

If you enjoyed this book and you want to have a complete guide on stock market investments, and trading strategies (including Swing and Day trading) then you will be interested in the complete collection of our author:

INVESTING AND TRADING STRATEGIES:
The Complete Crash Course with Proven Strategies to Become a Profitable Trader in the Financial Markets and Stop Living Paycheck to Paycheck.

If you love listening to audio books on-the-go, I have great news for you.

You Can Download the Audio Book Version of This Collection for FREE:

This audiobook is the complete box set of 11 books in the "Investing and trading Academy" series. They are collected in 4 main books: Stock Market Investing, Options Trading, Swing, and Day Trading Strategies. It can be yours for FREE.

Just by signing up for a FREE 30-day audible trial! See below for more details!

- FREE audible book copy of this book
- After the trial, you will get 1 credit each month to use on any audiobook
- Your credits automatically roll over to the next month if you don't use them
- Choose from Audible's 200,000 + titles
- Listen anywhere with the Audible app across multiple devices
- Make easy, no-hassle exchanges of any audiobook you don't love
- Keep your audiobooks forever, even if you cancel your membership

… and much more

Just scan the QR code below with your smartphone to get started right now FOR FREE!

For Audible US

For Audible UK

For Audible FR

For Audible DE

IPH BOOKS
INVESTING AND TRADING ACADEMY

Other Author's Works

by IPH Books - "Investing and trading Academy" Series

Stock Market Investing for Beginners

The Complete and Quick Guide to Becoming a Smart, Millionaire Investor by Recognizing the Best Investments. Learn How to Build and Diversify Your Investment Portfolio and Increase Your Wealth.

Stock Market Investing Strategies:

The Ultimate Guide to Learning and Recognizing the Factors that Affect the Stock Market. Discover How to Apply the Best Profitable Strategies in the Active and Passive Stock Market Without Fear.

Forex Trading for Beginners:

A Simple Guide to Find Out the Forex Trading Secrets to Make Money in Just a Few Weeks and Master Forex, CFDs, Commodities, and Cryptocurrencies Markets.

Options Trading for Beginners:

A QuickStart Guide to Maximizing Profit, Protect and Increase Your Invested Capital with Options Trading. Find Out How Swing and Day Trading Options Can Be Desirable and Profitable.

Options Trading Strategies:

A Beginner's Guide to Mastering the Financial Markets with these Best Options Trading Strategies, Made Simple, Generating Your Passive Income and Protecting Your Invested Capital.

IPH BOOKS
INVESTING AND TRADING ACADEMY

Technical Analysis for Your Profitable Trading:

Your Quick Beginner's Guide to Learn to Master Financial Markets Simply with Fibonacci, Japanese Candlesticks, and Price Action, Explained in Simple Terms.

Swing Trading for Beginners:

Simple Quick Guide to Learn How to Manage Your Trading Positions in Different Markets. Find Out How to Build Your Profitable Swing Trading Plan and Avoid Common Mistakes.

Swing Trading Strategies:

Learn the Best and Effective Strategies of the Pros with Elliot Waves. Get Started on Your Passive Income and Maximize Profits by Following Market Trends.

Day Trading for Beginners:

Everything You Need to Start Making Money Daily Right Away. Find Out All the Basics and Tips and Tricks to Become a Successful Day Trader.

Day trading Strategies:

A Quick Start Guide to Learning Technical Analysis and Becoming a Profitable Trader. Find Out Tips and Tricks with Simple Strategies to Build Your Next Passive Income Day-by-Day.

Trading for a Living:

A Complete Guide for Beginners and Intermediates on Money Management, Risk, Discipline, and the Psychology of Successful Trading. Everything You Need to Know to Get a Guaranteed Income for Life.

IPH BOOKS
INVESTING AND TRADING ACADEMY

by IPH Books - "Wealth Management Academy" Series

Credit Secrets: 3 Book in 1, Including An Unpublished Work:

The Complete Guide To Finding Out All the Secrets To Fix Your Credit Report and Boost Your Score. Learn How To Improve Your Finances and Have a Wealthy Lifestyle.

Credit Score Secrets

The Proven Guide To Increase Your Credit Score Once And For All. Manage Your Money, Your Personal Finance, And Your Debt To Achieve Financial Freedom Effortlessly.

Credit Repair Secrets:

Learn the Strategies and Techniques of Consultants and Credit Attoneys to Fix your Bad Debt and Improve your Business or Personal Finance. Including Dispute Letters.

IPH BOOKS
INVESTING AND TRADING ACADEMY

Author's Note

Thanks for reading my book. If you want to learn more about personal finance, investments, trading, and business, I suggest you follow my author page on Amazon. Through my books, I have decided to share with you the know-how that has allowed me to achieve my financial freedom, to accumulate wealth, and to live the life I want with my family.

My goal is to show you the path for reaching your targets, with useful and applicable information. Only you will be able to tread that path as I did… and now, I'm sharing what I know.

To your wealth!

Dave R. W. Graham

IPH BOOKS
INVESTING AND TRADING ACADEMY

CPSIA information can be obtained
at www.ICGtesting.com
Printed in the USA
BVHW092041250621
610374BV00002B/107

9 781914 409479